CW01095264

Prayers of
Blessing

**kevin
mayhew**

Anniversary

The joy of memory be yours today.
The joy of growth along the way.

Forgiveness be yours for failings past.
Fruit be yours that will always last.

May that day when you embarked
be also a day that in heaven is marked.

Baby

You are made in the likeness of the Good Birther,
little one.
May good grow in you.

You are made in the likeness of the
Compassionate Saviour, little one.
May compassion grow in you.

You are made in the likeness of the Creative Spirit,
little one.
May creativity grow in you.

You are made in the likeness of the Eternal Dance
of the Three, little one.
May the dance of life grow in you.

Battered People

Gentle Father,
bless these battered ones,
take the hurt out of their lives.

Tender Saviour,
bless these battered ones,
take the fear out of their lives.

Caressing Spirit,
bless these battered ones,
take the hardness out of their lives.

The blessing of acceptance be yours.
The blessing of forgiveness be yours.
The blessing of trust be yours.
The blessing of confidence be yours.
The blessing of decision be yours.
The blessing of growth be yours.
The blessing of eternal life be yours.

Car

May it bless the land it will travel on
and the earth that fuels it.

May it bless each person who enters it
and each person it passes:
the people on the roadside,
the people in the shops and workplaces,
the people in the public buildings and schools.

May each journey be an act of prayer,
a reflection of my journey through life.

Computer

Creator God, bless the surge that brings
this computer alive.
Saviour God, edit out the trash
and save that which is good.
Spirit of God, give to me ordered records,
creative thoughts and life-giving words.

As I programme my computer,
may I do it with your love.

As I summon words to screen,
may I do it with your mind.

As I edit, space and save,
may I do it with your eye.

As I surf for facts and pleasure,
may I do it with your heart.

Dentist

God bless my teeth
and the gums underneath.

May the dentist keep at bay
aggravating tooth decay.

May my teeth shine and gleam –
remind me, too, to keep them clean.

Discos

God give you:
the grace of movement,
the grace of beauty,
the grace of happiness,
the grace of conversation,
the grace of restraint,
the grace of self-forgetfulness,
the grace of being true to yourself.

Divorce

Grant me
acceptance of pain without bitterness,
grieving for loss without blame,
forgiveness for frailty without remorse,
renewal of trust without fear.

Exams

Designer of Truth, Protector from harm,
bless this exam to me.

Give me wisdom to know the nub of things,
memory to recall what is important,
clarity to express what I know,
and trust to leave the result with you.

Friends

Beauty of friendship grow between us;
friendship without guile,
friendship without malice,
friendship without striving.

Goodness of friendship grow between us;
friendship with insight,
friendship with faithfulness,
friendship with the light touch.

Garden

Here
may the earth be full of health,
may the plants be full of sap,
may the flowers be full of colour,
may the birds be full of chirps,
may the pets be full of wags,
may the people be full of joy.

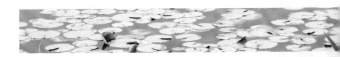

Gym

God bless the gym,
and every limb.

God bless the pool,
make it not too cool.

God bless my body,
may it not be shoddy.

Holidays

Blessing of discovery be yours,
and blessing of rest.

Blessing of scenery be yours,
and blessing of sleep.

Blessing of meeting be yours,
and blessing of solitude.

Blessing of fun be yours,
and blessing of thought.

Blessing of change be yours,
and blessing of homecoming.

Infertility

Birther of Life,
bless the swarming sperm.

Spirit of Life,
bless the welcoming egg.

Saviour of Life,
quicken the barren womb.

Three of All-Fertile Love,
make our union teem with life that has no end.

Joining up – (the Armed Services)

May you have
truth in your hearts,
strength in your arms,
consistency in your tongues,
nobility in your deeds,
mercy in your being.

Kitchen

Jesus, who helped Mary in the kitchen,
may your Spirit fill all who work here.

May the washing-up be done in a spirit of service,
may the cooking be done with a desire to nourish.
And may there be a glory amid the clatter.

Lottery Win

Good be on you, gift from heaven.
Restraint be on you, gift from heaven.
Wisdom be on you, gift from heaven.
Generosity be on you, gift from heaven,
lest you become a gift from hell.

Motorcyclist

God bless your steed,
God bless your speed,
Christ meet your need.

By the Spirit be led,
with angels overhead,
until you reach your bed.

Mountain Bike

God speed to you.
Good movement to you.
Fine balance to you.

Power of air to you.
Power of wheel to you.
Power of frame to you.

Good ups to you.
And also good downs.

Next-Door Neighbours

I don't know much about next door,
and I'm not sure I like what I know.
But in the name of Jesus I will bless you:

Some time, may a smile replace that sour face.
Some day, may the garden start to look happy.
Whatever goes on inside,
may God somehow get inside you.

Office

Bless this little space that so many people
come through.
May the papers be kept in order,
may unnecessary things come to their end.
May each telephone ring be met
with a welcoming voice.
When something breaks down, may I rise up.
Bless the people who come into this space.

Parents

May the Three of Limitless Love
replenish your stock of love.

May those you care for not take you for granted.

God give you grace to
listen to your loved ones,
play with your loved ones,
weep with your loved ones,
confront your loved ones,
explain things to your loved ones,
and then to give them away as a blessing
to the world.

Pets

God care for you, my pet,
keep you well and fit.

May your life on this earth be blest,
and then may you go to your rest.

Friends may we be for a while.
Always bring to mind a smile.

May you be kept content.
Thieves may God prevent.

Places

God who sweeps the sky and earth

make sacred the landscapes where we live and die;

grant them

the blessing of forgiving memory,

the blessing of victorious faith,

the blessing of constant prayer.

Purse

God, take my purse,

and be its nurse.

God, take my card,

and be its guard.

God, take me in hand.

I'll understand.

Questionnaires

God save me from questionnaires that are much
ado about nothing.
Give me grace to refuse them,
or else humour if I have to complete them.

God bless the questionnaires that help folk
better serve the world.
Give me grace to attentively fill them in,
or at least the strength to send them off with love.

Room

God bless the room in which I sleep,
may it not be an untidy heap.

Give something of beauty for my eyes to see,
clean without and within please let it be.

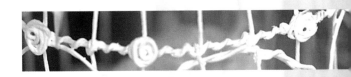

Room-Mates

May the Three of Limitless Love free you to:
enjoy the other's company,
accept the other's pain,
express your needs,
forgive from your heart,
that you may flower as persons.

Sport Competitions

The strength of an ox be yours,
the speed of a gazelle be yours,
the suppleness of a fish be yours,
the reach of a bird be yours –
the wreath of God around you
and gold everlasting.

Stepchildren

A family of friends to draw round you,
a family to cherish you and introduce you to new things.

The family of God to draw round you,
Mary, the mother of Jesus,
Joseph in his workplace,
opening heaven's gates to welcome you.

The Tongue

Guardian of Truth, God of Love,

when my tongue runs away with me,

run after it and bring it back;

when my tongue runs others down,

pick it up and put it in its place;

when my tongue blesses others,

bless it to me.

Toys

Bless the stuffed toys
that make no noise.

Bless the ones that speak
and make me shriek.

Bless the ones that move
and make folk rove.

May these toys do well,
then their stories I'll tell.

Tragedy

The blessing of acceptance be yours,
the blessing of forgiveness be yours,
the blessing of gentleness be yours,
the blessing of resilience be yours,
the blessing of eternal life be yours.

POCKET RACER

_TV_

God make the TV
a blessing to me.

When there's horrible stuff
may I turn the switch off.

When there's too much choice
may I listen to your voice.

May the people in the soap
not give up hope.

When celebrities show off
may we say 'now that's enough'.

May the good world out there
also get on air.

What in heaven is seen,
may it get on screen.

Unto You

Unto you, O Lord, be praise
for every flower that ever grew,
every bird that ever flew,
every wind that ever blew.

Unto you, O Lord, be praise
for every flake of virgin snow,
every place where humans go,
every joy and every woe.

Unto you, O Lord, be praise
for every life that shall be born,
every heart that shall be torn,
every day and every dawn.

Echoes an early Irish prayer.

Victims

The Divine Gift come into your loss.
The Divine Peace come into your dread.
The Divine Hope come into your despair.
The Divine Helper come to your aid.

Work

Be in the humdrum,
be in the highs.

Be in the setbacks,
be in the skies.

Be in the interruptions,
be in the cries.

Be in the people,
be in the eyes.

Xmas Tree

May the branches that point upwards
lead us to worship the Creator
who came from heaven to be born as a child.

May the needles that fall to the ground
remind us of the needs of the poor
and those at the bottom of the social pile.

May the decorations that brighten this dark season
inspire us to celebrate it with thoughtfulness and joy.

Youth

God help you to
run straight,
bear failure,
be true,
make friends,
honour the other,
explore the world,
give your best,
reverence your Creator.

Zeal of God

Zeal of God, fill my being.
Truth of God, light my way.
Peace of God, redeem my past.
Love of God, come in today.

First published in 2005 by

KEVIN MAYHEW LTD
Buxhall, Stowmarket, Suffolk, IP14 3BW
E-mail: info@kevinmayhewltd.com
Website: www.kevinmayhew.com

9 8 7 6 5 4 3 2 1 0

ISBN 1 84417 418 2
Catalogue No. 1500809

Designed by Chris Coe
Edited by Marian Reid

Printed and bound in China

Ray Simpson is a co-founder of the worldwide
Community of Aidan and Hilda and is its first guardian.
He lives on Lindisfarne, where the Community has a
retreat and guesthouse: The Open Gate, Holy Island,
Berwick-upon-Tweed, TD15 2SD.
The Community's website is www.aidan.org.uk